INSIDE THE NFL

CAROLINA PANTHERS

by Luke Hanlon

Abdo & Daughters
MIDDLE GRADE NONFICTION

An imprint of Abdo Publishing
abdobooks.com

ABDOBOOKS.COM

Published by Abdo Publishing, a division of ABDO, PO Box 398166, Minneapolis, Minnesota 55439.

Printed in China.
052025
092025

Cover Photos: Cliff Welch/Icon Sportswire/Getty Images (Bryce Young); Craig Jones/Getty Images Sport/Getty Images (Julius Peppers)
Interior Photos: Streeter Lecka/Getty Images Sport/Getty Images, 4–5, 7, 53, 56, 61 (top right); Joe Robbins/Getty Images Sport/Getty Images, 6; Grant Halverson/Getty Images Sport/Getty Images, 8, 52, 61 (bottom left); Scott Cunningham/Getty Images Sport/Getty Images, 10, 61 (bottom right); Bob Leverone/AP Images, 11; Abdo Publishing, 12–13; Mark Elias/AP Images, 14–15; Paul Spinelli/NFL Photos/AP Images, 16; Al Messerschmidt Archive/AP Images, 17; Al Bello/Getty Images Sport/Getty Images, 18; Focus on Sport/Getty Images Sport/Getty Images, 19, 28; Ruth Fremson/AP Images, 20; Alan Marler/AP Images, 21; David Stluka/AP Images, 22, 45; Otto Greule Jr./Getty Images Sport/Getty Images, 23; Andy Lyons/Allsport/Getty Images Sport/Getty Images, 24, 25, 60 (bottom left); Stephen Dunn/Allsport/Getty Images Sport/Getty Images, 26–27; Mike McCarn/AP Images, 29; Craig Jones/Allsport/Getty Images Sport/Getty Images, 30; Craig Jones/Getty Images Sport/Getty Images, 31, 38–39, 60 (top left); Drew Hallowell/Getty Images Sport/Getty Images, 32–33; Charles Rex Arbogast/AP Images, 34, 63; Mark J. Terrill/AP Images, 35; Brian Bahr/Getty Images Sport/Getty Images, 36, 60 (bottom right); G. Newman Lowrance/AP Images, 37; Jed Jacobsohn/Getty Images Sport/Getty Images, 40–41; Rick Havner/AP Images, 42, 46; Al Messerschmidt/Getty Images Sport/Getty Images, 43; Andy Lyons/Getty Images Sport/Getty Images, 44, 60 (top right); Nell Redmond/AP Images, 47; Dave Martin/AP Images, 48; Ralph Freso/AP Images, 49; David J. Phillip/AP Images, 50–51, 61 (top left); Patrick Smith/Getty Images Sport/Getty Images, 54; Abbie Parr/Getty Images Sport/Getty Images, 55; Jonathan Bachman/Getty Images Sports/Getty Images, 57; Shutterstock Images, 58; Chris Graythen/Getty Images Sport/Getty Images, 59

Editor: Rebecca Higgins
Series Designer: Laura Graphenteen
Production Designer: Katharine Hale

Library of Congress Control Number: 2024948487

Publisher's Cataloging-in-Publication Data

Names: Hanlon, Luke, author.
Title: Carolina Panthers / by Luke Hanlon
Description: Minneapolis, Minnesota: Abdo Publishing, 2026 | Series: Inside the NFL | Includes online resources and index.
Identifiers: ISBN 9781098296667 (lib. bdg.) | ISBN 9798384919186 (ebook)
Subjects: LCSH: Carolina Panthers (Football team)--Juvenile literature. | National Football League--Juvenile literature. | Football teams--Juvenile literature. | American football--Juvenile literature.
Classification: DDC 796.33264--dc23

CONTENTS

Luke Kuechly, *right*, tackles a New Orleans Saint on December 22, 2013.

CHAPTER 1

TACKLING MACHINE

THE NEW ORLEANS SAINTS STRUGGLED TO GET ANY OFFENSE GOING. Luke Kuechly was a big reason why. The Carolina Panthers' middle linebacker flew around the field. The Saints ran a pass-heavy offense, and they tried to move the ball with quick throws to running backs or tight ends. Once those players caught the ball, Kuechly often greeted them with a crushing tackle.

The Panthers were hosting the Saints during Week 16 of the 2013 National Football League (NFL) season. Games between the division rivals always carried high stakes, but this one was even more important. A win for either team would clinch a spot in the playoffs and almost certainly secure the National Football Conference (NFC) South division title as well. If the Panthers won, they would be heading to the postseason for the first time in five years.

Both defenses were aggressive in the pivotal matchup. At halftime, Carolina led 7–6. When the teams retook the field in the second half, rain began pouring down at Carolina's Bank of America Stadium. The sloppy weather conditions suited Kuechly's skills perfectly.

DEFENSIVE GENIUS

Coming into the 2012 draft, the Panthers already had two former first-round picks starting at linebacker with Thomas Davis and Jon Beason. With the ninth pick, Carolina had an opportunity to pick a top prospect. Many thought the team would address a position other than linebacker. However, the Panthers' front office quickly put Kuechly at the top of its list. While at Boston College, Kuechly showcased elite athleticism and a rare ability to recognize what the offense was going to do.

Kuechly was still available when the ninth pick came. The Panthers were thrilled to select him. He quickly showed that Carolina made the right pick. In his

Kuechly runs during the 2012 NFL Combine, where scouts assess the skills of potential draft picks.

Kuechly led the NFL with 164 tackles in 2012.

Kuechly grabbed 18 interceptions in his eight years with Carolina.

first season, Kuechly led the league in tackles and claimed the NFL Defensive Rookie of the Year Award. The linebacker's teammates were amazed by his dominance. Panthers head coach Ron Rivera would sometimes have to take Kuechly off the field in practice so the offense could successfully rehearse a play without him blowing it up. "He was the most physically gifted guy on the field at any time, and he knew every play you were going to run," Panthers tight end Greg Olsen said.

"HE WAS THE MOST PHYSICALLY GIFTED GUY ON THE FIELD AT ANY TIME, AND HE KNEW EVERY PLAY YOU WERE GOING TO RUN."

—GREG OLSEN ON LUKE KUECHLY

By his second season, Kuechly helped anchor the Carolina defense alongside the veteran Davis. Kuechly continued to rack up tackles and break up passes while helping the Panthers go on an eight-game win streak in the middle of the year. But the Saints ended that streak in Week 13. Two weeks later, with a playoff spot on the line, the Panthers would face New Orleans. Carolina wanted revenge.

MAKING HISTORY

In the Week 16 game against the Saints, Carolina's defense wreaked havoc. Each time Kuechly wrapped up a New Orleans player for a short gain, the home fans serenaded him by yelling, "Luuuuuke!" His name echoed around the stadium dozens of times as the Saints' offense struggled to respond.

With 4:34 left in the third quarter, the rain continued to soak the field and the players. Trailing 10–6, the Saints had the ball. If they could move it down the field for a touchdown, they would take the lead. On a third-and-10 play, New Orleans quarterback Drew Brees

Kuechly intercepts the New Orleans Saints.

dropped back to pass. Carolina's pass rush charged, shrinking the pocket for Brees. Thinking fast, the star quarterback stepped up and fired the ball toward the middle of the field. Kuechly was ready. The linebacker dove in front of Brees' target and intercepted the pass at midfield.

Kuechly continued to make the Saints sweat. Midway through the fourth quarter, Kuechly stuffed Saints running back Mark Ingram at the line of scrimmage for no gain. He racked up his 24th tackle, which tied the NFL record for the most tackles in a game. Kuechly's relentless play helped the Panthers eke out a 17–13 win and secure a spot in the playoffs. His tough performances established him as one of the league's best players at only 22 years old.

CAREER CUT SHORT

Luke Kuechly remained a powerhouse throughout his career. Every season he played with Carolina, he recorded at least 100 tackles. And starting in 2013, Kuechly made the Pro Bowl for seven years in a row. He probably would've reached more Pro Bowls, but Kuechly missed seven games in his career due to concussions. After the 2019 season, Kuechly still desperately wanted to play the sport he loved. But he decided to retire at 28 because of the long-term risk of suffering additional head injuries.

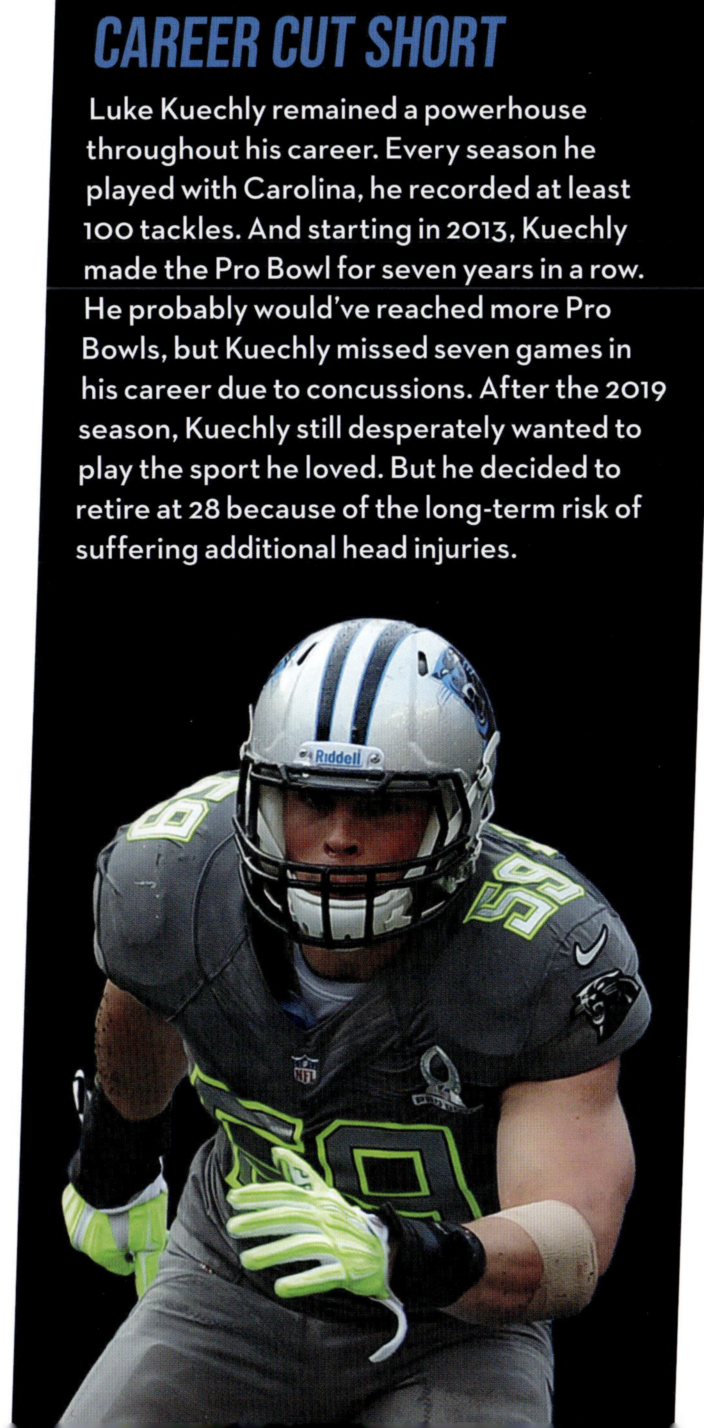

NFL TEAMS MAP

NFC EAST

DALLAS COWBOYS

NEW YORK GIANTS

PHILADELPHIA EAGLES

WASHINGTON COMMANDERS

NFC WEST

ARIZONA CARDINALS

LOS ANGELES RAMS

SAN FRANCISCO 49ERS

SEATTLE SEAHAWKS

NFC NORTH

CHICAGO BEARS

DETROIT LIONS

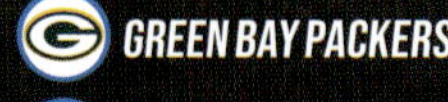
GREEN BAY PACKERS

MINNESOTA VIKINGS

NFC SOUTH

ATLANTA FALCONS

CAROLINA PANTHERS

NEW ORLEANS SAINTS

TAMPA BAY BUCCANEERS

AFC

AFC EAST

- BUFFALO BILLS
- MIAMI DOLPHINS
- NEW ENGLAND PATRIOTS
- NEW YORK JETS

AFC WEST

- DENVER BRONCOS
- KANSAS CITY CHIEFS
- LAS VEGAS RAIDERS
- LOS ANGELES CHARGERS

AFC NORTH

- BALTIMORE RAVENS
- CINCINNATI BENGALS
- CLEVELAND BROWNS
- PITTSBURGH STEELERS

AFC SOUTH

- HOUSTON TEXANS
-  INDIANAPOLIS COLTS
-  JACKSONVILLE JAGUARS
-  TENNESSEE TITANS

Jerry Richardson holds up a Panthers helmet in 1993.

CHAPTER 2

CAROLINA'S TEAM

Jerry Richardson was born and raised in North Carolina. He went on to play wide receiver for the Baltimore Colts. In 1959, he won an NFL championship with the team. Decades later, Richardson wanted to bring an NFL team to the Carolinas. In December 1987, he submitted an official bid to have a Carolina team join the league.

One of the first things Richardson needed to do was find a site for the team's stadium. He considered locating the team in either North or South Carolina. In 1989, Richardson announced that he would build a stadium in Charlotte, North Carolina. The city sits on the state's southern border, so South Carolinian fans could easily travel to games.

Carolinians were thrilled that they might have a pro football team. The governors of North and

Richardson, *right*, stands at the podium during a celebration of the Carolinas getting an NFL team on October 26, 1993.

South Carolina publicly supported the bid. Starting in 1989, the Carolinas hosted NFL preseason games to show the league that the area would have dedicated fans. In a three-year span, Chapel Hill and Raleigh in North Carolina, as well as Columbia in South Carolina, hosted games. Despite the games featuring teams from other parts of the country, sellout crowds attended each one.

These turnouts impressed NFL owners. By 1993, Charlotte and four other cities were being considered for

BECOMING THE PANTHERS

One of the most important parts of creating an expansion team is coming up with a name. Many new franchises hold votes, letting their fans have a say in what the team is called. Jerry Richardson didn't do that. His son Mark Richardson was the team's president. The younger Richardson chose the name Panthers. "It's a name our family thought signifies what we thought a team should be: powerful, sleek, and strong," Mark Richardson said.

The Panthers have played in the same stadium since 1996.

one of the league's two expansion teams. On June 3 of that year, Richardson announced that the stadium in Charlotte would hold 72,300 fans. Even without the guarantee of a team, fans snapped up 41,632 season tickets in a day. When the league decided on its expansion teams in October 1993, all 28 owners voted in favor of Charlotte getting a team.

BUILDING A TEAM FROM SCRATCH

Along with the Panthers, the Jacksonville Jaguars also entered the NFL in the 1995 season. Before playing any games, the two teams participated in an expansion draft to start building their rosters.

The NFL required each of the 28 established teams to make six players on their roster available for the Panthers and the Jaguars. The new teams each selected more than 30 players that way. They filled out the rest of their rosters through the normal NFL Draft and free agency process. There was one free agent that Panthers head coach Dom Capers desperately wanted. Capers had previously served as the defensive coordinator for the Pittsburgh Steelers, and he wanted Carolina to have a feared defense right away. He pleaded with the Panthers' front office to sign Sam Mills. Capers viewed the four-time Pro Bowl linebacker as a leader he could build his team around. Mills left the New Orleans Saints to sign with the Panthers before the 1995 season.

Then in that year's draft, the team strengthened its offense and defense. The Jaguars had won a coin toss to get the first pick in the expansion draft, so the NFL granted the first pick in the regular draft to the Panthers. But Carolina traded the selection to the Cincinnati Bengals in exchange for the fifth pick and a second-round pick. Carolina then used its fifth pick, which was also the team's first-ever regular NFL Draft selection, on quarterback Kerry Collins. He had just led Penn State to an undefeated season. However, when Carolina played the Atlanta Falcons in its first game, veteran quarterback Frank Reich earned the starting job.

Sam Mills had played in the NFL for nine seasons before signing with the Panthers.

Kerry Collins, *right*, was the second quarterback selected in the 1995 draft.

ROUGH START

Throughout NFL history, expansion teams often struggled in their first season in the league. Early in the 1995 season, the Panthers followed that trend. After a Week 1 overtime loss to the Falcons, Carolina got blown out in its next two games. Following a bye week, Capers turned to Collins as the starting quarterback. While the next two games were closer, the Panthers fell to 0–5.

In Week 7, the Panthers hosted the New York Jets. Carolina's offense struggled early in the game. In the second quarter, the Jets sacked Collins for a safety. Then he threw interceptions on the next two drives, with the Jets returning one of them for a touchdown. Another loss seemed inevitable for the Panthers. However, momentum shifted later in the quarter. With the Panthers trailing 12–6, Mills burst through the Jets offensive line and intercepted a shovel pass. He ran past the Jets quarterback then followed a lead blocker to return the pick 36 yards, scoring a touchdown. Mills's teammates and coaches were amazed that the 36-year-old made it all the way to the end zone. "I told him he looked like he was 25 again out there on that run," Capers said. Carolina kicker John Kasay's extra-point kick was good and gave the Panthers a lead at halftime.

Mills celebrates his touchdown against the Jets.

In the locker room, belief spread among the Carolina players that they could win. The Panthers never lost the lead against the Jets and clinched their first NFL victory. Mills's pick six was a major turning point for Carolina's season. It sparked a four-game win streak for the Panthers. They went on to win seven of their last 11 games of

"I TOLD HIM HE LOOKED LIKE HE WAS 25 AGAIN OUT THERE ON THAT RUN."

—DOM CAPERS ON SAM MILLS

Dom Capers, *left*, and linebacker Lamar Lathon, *right*, celebrate the first win in Carolina's history.

the season, finishing with a 7–9 record. No NFL expansion team had ever won that many games in its first season.

MAJOR UPGRADES

Heading into the 1996 season, the Panthers signed multiple free agents to upgrade their roster. Outside linebacker Kevin Greene had played for Capers in Pittsburgh and led the league in sacks in 1994. Greene left the Steelers hoping to get more playing time with Carolina. The Panthers also signed cornerback Eric Davis, who was coming off an All-Pro season with the San Francisco 49ers. On the same day Carolina brought in Davis, the team signed tight end Wesley Walls from the Saints.

Walls became Collins's favorite target, leading the Panthers in receptions and receiving touchdowns in 1996. The Panthers also selected wide receiver Muhsin Muhammad in the second round of the 1996 draft to give Collins another reliable pass-catcher. The offensive additions helped Collins improve from his rookie year and earn a spot in the Pro Bowl.

Kevin Greene recorded 160 sacks in his 15 seasons as a pro.

Carolina's defense remained the team's greatest strength. At 37 years old, Mills made the All-Pro team after leading a defense that allowed the second-fewest points in the league. Meanwhile, Greene led the team in sacks. And Davis tied with teammate Chad Cota for most interceptions on the Panthers.

Coming into Week 11 of the 1996 season, the Panthers had lost two games in a row, falling to 5–4. Carolina beat the New York

Eric Davis grabbed five interceptions in 1996.

Giants that week. The 27–17 victory kicked off a seven-game win streak to end the season. Finishing with a 12–4 record, the Panthers won their division.

The win meant Carolina earned a first-round bye in the playoffs and would host its first playoff game. But experts expected the Dallas Cowboys to beat the Panthers on their home field. After all, the Cowboys were the defending Super Bowl champs. That prediction looked accurate as Collins threw an interception on the first drive of the game. But Collins recovered quickly. On the next drive, he found a wide-open Walls in the end zone for a 1-yard touchdown to take the lead. Early in the second quarter, Collins threaded a pass to wide receiver Willie Green in tight coverage for another score, putting the Panthers up 14–3.

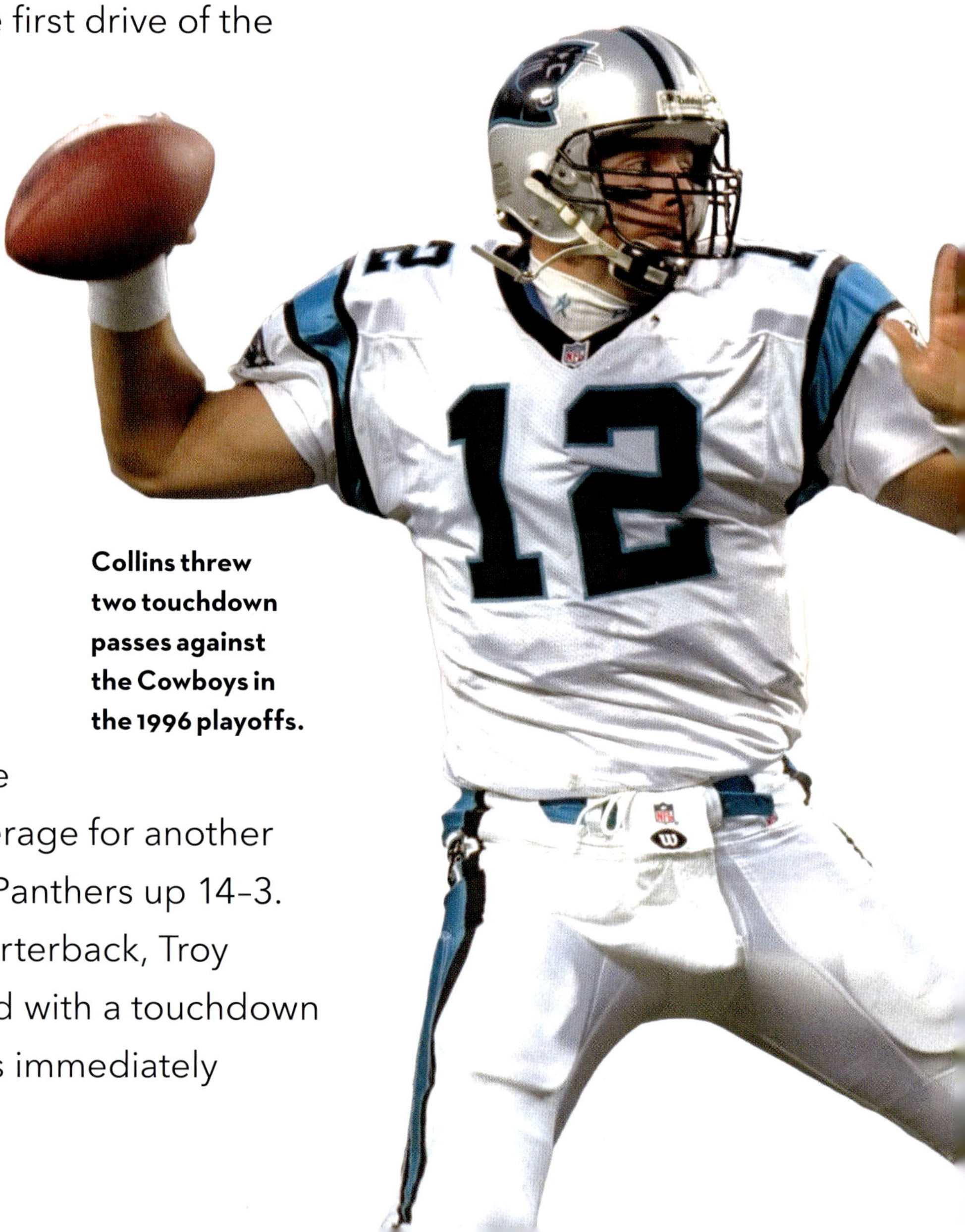

Collins threw two touchdown passes against the Cowboys in the 1996 playoffs.

Dallas's star quarterback, Troy Aikman, responded with a touchdown drive. The Panthers immediately

Mills returns an interception against the Cowboys in the 1996 playoffs.

stepped up their defense. Aikman threw three interceptions, including a pick by Mills with 1:19 left in the game. The Panthers sealed a 26–17 win.

After the team's first playoff win, Carolina faced the Green Bay Packers in the conference championship game. The Panthers took an early 7–0 lead, but the Packers proved to be too much for Carolina to handle. Green Bay won 30–13 on its way to becoming Super Bowl champion.

Panthers running back Fred Lane scored seven rushing touchdowns in 1997.

CHAPTER 3

ON THE PROWL

HEADING INTO THE 1997 SEASON, CAROLINA'S TRAINING CAMP WAS filled with optimism. Many of the team's 1996 division-winning players had returned. However, when fans attended practices in July 1997, they couldn't take their eyes off undrafted rookie running back Fred Lane. He stole the show from veteran stars such as Sam Mills, Eric Davis, and Wesley Walls. It seemed as if every time Lane touched the ball, he broke a tackle and ran for a huge gain.

Coming into training camp, few expected Lane would even make the team. Veteran running back Anthony Johnson had led the 1996 Panthers in rushing and remained on the roster. Carolina also had its 1996 first-round pick, running back Tim Biakabutuka. But Lane's impressive camp earned him a spot on the team. By Week 10, he became the Panthers' starting running back. Lane finished the season with a team-leading 809 rushing yards and seven rushing touchdowns.

Lane turned out to be the highlight of Carolina's 1997 season. While it wasn't publicly known, Kerry Collins was struggling with alcohol addiction throughout the season. The disease affected his relationship with his teammates. He led the league in interceptions thrown.

Kerry Collins threw a league-high 21 interceptions in 1997.

At the same time, Carolina's defense took a step back. The Panthers finished 7–9 and missed the playoffs.

The 1997 season also marked the end of Mills's career. After 12 years in the NFL, including three years with the Panthers, Mills retired at 38 years old. While he joined Carolina's coaching staff for the 1998 season, the Panthers missed his presence on the field. A once dominant defense declined into one of the worst in the league. Meanwhile, after starting 0–4, the Panthers tried to trade Collins. When no other teams showed interest, Carolina released him. After finishing the season 4–12, the Panthers fired Dom Capers. Just like that, the core that led Carolina to its early success was gone.

LOCAL LEGEND

The Panthers kicked off their 2001 season by defeating the Minnesota Vikings. However, Carolina went on to lose 15 games in a row, setting the NFL single-season record for longest losing streak. The one bright spot from that many losses was receiving the second pick in the 2002 NFL Draft.

Many draft experts considered Julius Peppers to be the best prospect available that year. He turned heads playing high school football in

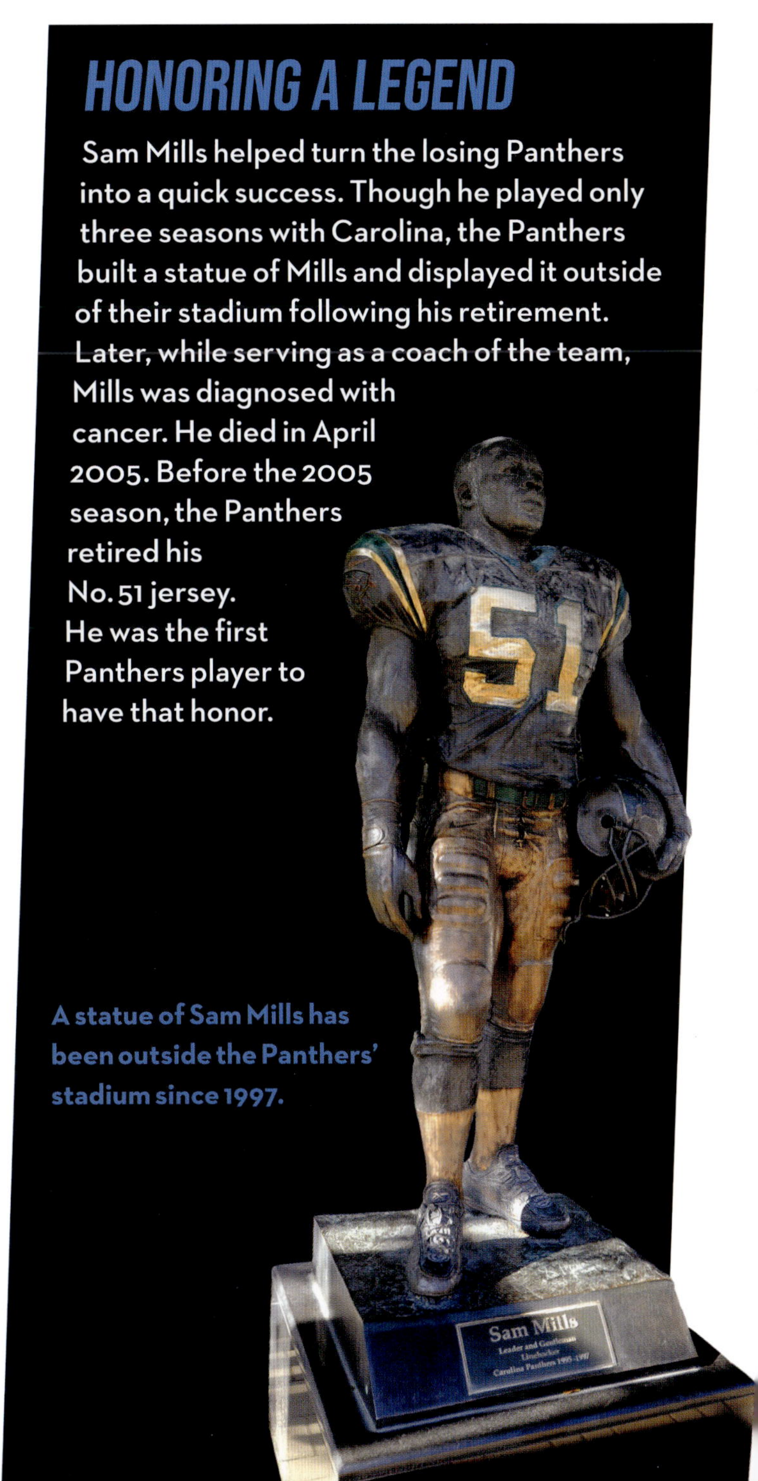

HONORING A LEGEND

Sam Mills helped turn the losing Panthers into a quick success. Though he played only three seasons with Carolina, the Panthers built a statue of Mills and displayed it outside of their stadium following his retirement. Later, while serving as a coach of the team, Mills was diagnosed with cancer. He died in April 2005. Before the 2005 season, the Panthers retired his No. 51 jersey. He was the first Panthers player to have that honor.

A statue of Sam Mills has been outside the Panthers' stadium since 1997.

Bailey, North Carolina. The 6-foot-5, 240-pound Peppers could outrun defenders as a running back and overpower opponents as a defensive lineman. When football season ended, Peppers thrived on the basketball court. He had always dreamed of playing basketball at the University of North Carolina. He ended up doing just that while also excelling in football for the Tar Heels.

Julius Peppers averaged 5.7 points per game during his basketball career at North Carolina.

The Houston Texans chose quarterback David Carr with the first pick in the draft. With the second pick, the Panthers selected Peppers and kept him in his home state. It didn't take long for Peppers to adapt to the NFL. In his second pro game, Peppers recorded his first sack after shedding two blockers. He went on to rack up two more sacks and force a fumble in that game. The rookie helped Carolina seal a 31–7 win over the Detroit Lions.

Peppers won the NFL Defensive Rookie of the Year Award in 2002.

Peppers fit perfectly into new head coach John Fox's strategy. Before getting the Panthers job, Fox served as the defensive coordinator for the New York Giants. His main goal when taking over a team coming off a 1–15 season was to make the Panthers tougher. Drafting Peppers certainly helped.

The Panthers allowed 28 total points in their first three games in 2002 and started the season 3–0. However, the defense couldn't completely carry the team's underwhelming offense. After the hot start, Carolina lost eight straight games and finished the season with a 7–9 record. The team missed the playoffs. Throughout the season, many of Carolina's fans loved watching Peppers. The Associated Press named him Defensive Rookie of the Year. With a tough defense, the Panthers headed into the 2003 season looking for a player to lead their offense.

Quarterback Jake Delhomme (17) threw 19 touchdowns in 2003.

UNLIKELY STARTER

Before the 2003 season, the Panthers signed Jake Delhomme as their backup quarterback. At that point, the 28-year-old had played more games in European football leagues than in the NFL. Delhomme went undrafted in 1997 and then signed with the New Orleans Saints. In between stints in Europe, he started two games for the Saints and played in six total.

Rodney Peete opened the season as the Panthers' starting quarterback. In Week 1 against the Jacksonville Jaguars, Peete completed only four pass attempts for 19 yards before halftime. The Panthers trailed 14–0. Fox decided to have Delhomme take

over for the second half. On Delhomme's first drive, he rifled a pass between three defenders to find Muhsin Muhammad for a 13-yard touchdown.

After a back-and-forth second half, the Panthers trailed 23–18. They got the ball near midfield with 3:34 to play. Delhomme marched Carolina down the field. With only 22 seconds left, the Panthers faced fourth-and-11 at Jacksonville's 12-yard line. Wide receiver Ricky Proehl leaped in the air to catch a perfect spiral from Delhomme in the end zone. The Panthers claimed a 24–23 win over Jacksonville. Pulling off the unlikely comeback earned Delhomme the starting job for Week 2.

Delhomme didn't always light up the stat sheet. But he always seemed to find a way to deliver when it mattered most. In three games, Delhomme led the Panthers on game-winning drives in overtime. These successes helped the Panthers jump to a 6–1 record. Delhomme ended up leading the league with five fourth-quarter comebacks and seven game-winning drives. His heroics helped the Panthers win their division and secure a spot in the playoffs.

Steve Smith's score against the Rams was only the second game-winning touchdown in double overtime in NFL playoff history.

THE BIG GAME

The Panthers started their playoff run with a comfortable 29–10 win against the Dallas Cowboys. In the divisional round, the Panthers traveled to St. Louis to take on the Rams. Carolina was used to coming back from fourth-quarter deficits. However, this time it was the Rams who made the comeback. Trailing 23–12, St. Louis rallied in the final three minutes to tie the Panthers. The teams continued the battle in overtime.

Both teams missed game-winning field-goal attempts in overtime. The game headed into double overtime. The Panthers faced third-and-14 on the first play of double overtime. With time to throw, Delhomme zipped the ball 20 yards down the middle of the

DeShaun Foster dives into the end zone during Super Bowl XXXVIII.

field to Steve Smith. A Rams defender dove at the wide receiver's feet but came up short. Then Smith sprinted past two more defenders on his way to a 69-yard touchdown to win the game. "I've never seen a game quite like that, let alone be involved in one," Fox said after the win.

A week later, the Panthers traveled to Philadelphia. Carolina gave up only three points, beating the Eagles 14–3 and earning its first trip to the Super Bowl. The Panthers faced off against the

"I'VE NEVER SEEN A GAME QUITE LIKE THAT, LET ALONE BE INVOLVED IN ONE."

—JOHN FOX

New England Patriots. The Patriots had won the Super Bowl two years earlier in part due to the emergence of young quarterback Tom Brady. Like Delhomme, Brady had started the 2001 season as a backup. Once New England's starter suffered an injury, Brady took over and never lost the starting job. Heading into Super Bowl XXXVIII after the 2003 season, Brady and the Patriots were on a 14-game winning streak. Experts predicted that New England would easily beat the Panthers.

Both offenses struggled early in the game. Delhomme dropped a perfect 39-yard touchdown pass into Smith's hands to tie the game 7–7. However, by the start of the fourth quarter, the Panthers trailed 21–10. Just as they had done all season, the team rallied. DeShaun Foster ran 33 yards for a touchdown to cut the deficit to five points. Then Panthers defensive back Reggie Howard intercepted Brady in the end zone. Three plays later, Delhomme used play-action, and it completely fooled the Patriots' defense. Two defensive backs lost Muhammad on a deep route, and Delhomme uncorked the ball more than 50 yards to connect with the open receiver. Muhammad then sprinted all the way for an 85-yard touchdown. The longest pass play in Super Bowl history gave the Panthers the lead.

Muhsin Muhammad caught four passes for 140 yards during Super Bowl XXXVIII.

Panthers players and coaches watch from the sideline as Adam Vinatieri's game-winning field goal sails through the uprights to clinch Super Bowl XXXVIII for the Patriots.

Brady wasn't fazed. He responded with a touchdown drive to give the Patriots a 29–22 lead with 2:51 to go. Delhomme then diced up the New England defense on the ensuing drive. In a little more than a minute, he led the Panthers down to New England's 12-yard line. Under pressure, he delivered a pass to an open Proehl in the end zone, and the Panthers tied the game with 1:08 left.

It seemed that the Panthers were going to end their season with another fourth-quarter comeback. But Brady had other ideas. He drove the Patriots down to Carolina's 23-yard line and set up Adam Vinatieri's game-winning field goal. The Panthers' quest for a Super Bowl title had come up just short with a 32–29 loss.

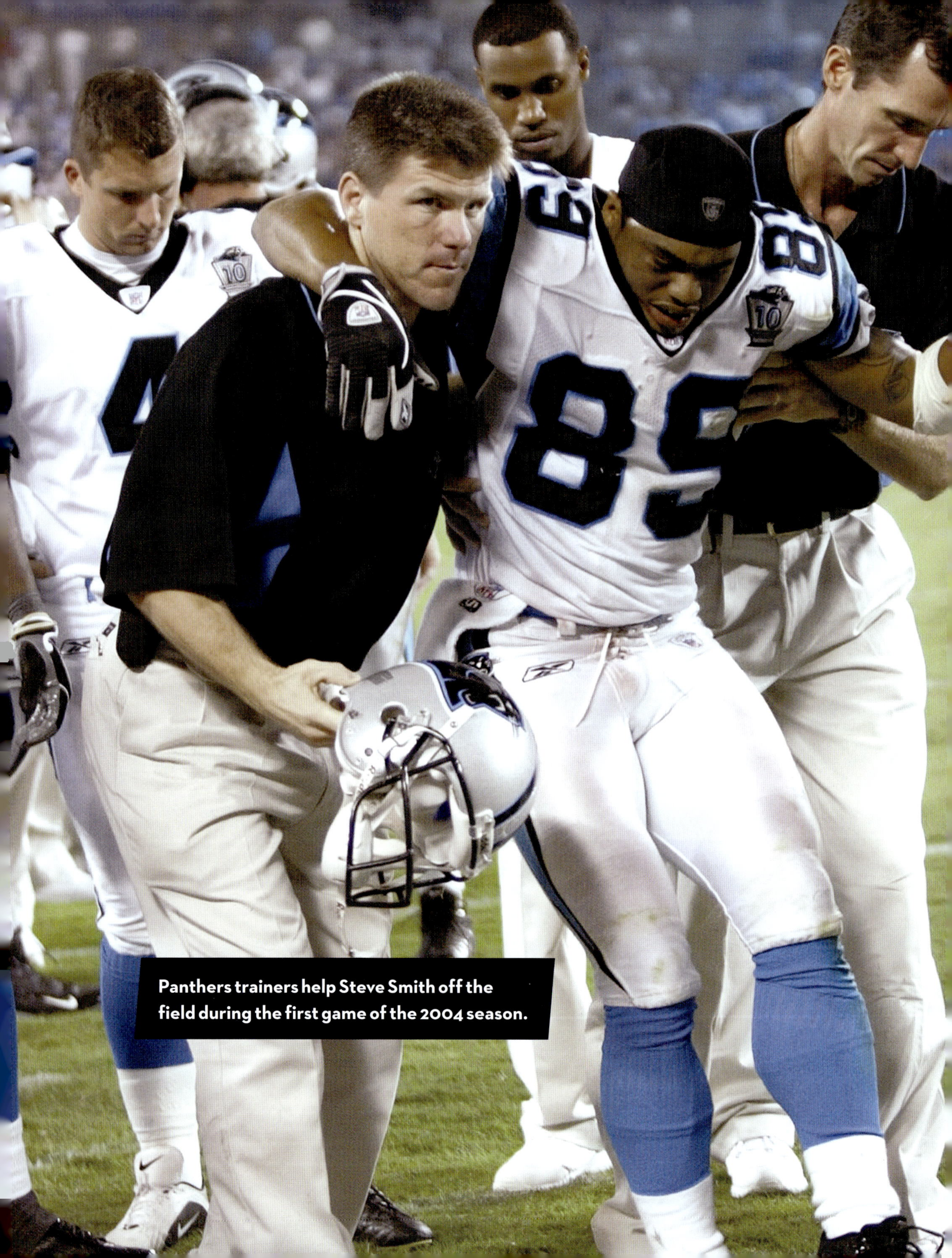

Panthers trainers help Steve Smith off the field during the first game of the 2004 season.

CHAPTER 4

NEXT PLAYER UP

THE PANTHERS' HOPES FOR BUILDING ON THEIR SUPER BOWL appearance quickly came undone in the 2004 season. In Week 1, star wide receiver Steve Smith broke his leg. He missed the rest of the year. Days after the game, Pro Bowl running back Stephen Davis suffered a knee injury in practice. Backup running back DeShaun Foster had enjoyed a breakout year in 2003 and seemed poised to emerge as a star with Davis out. However, Foster broke his collarbone in Week 4 and was out the remainder of the season.

Those injuries took a toll on the Panthers, and the team started the season 1–7. Then in Week 10, Carolina fell behind the San Francisco 49ers 17–0. Without Davis or Foster, the Panthers needed other playmakers to step up. Fortunately, Muhsin Muhammad was still healthy, and

Delhomme found him for three touchdowns in the second half. The Panthers rallied to win 37–27 and end a six-game losing streak.

That win sparked new life into Carolina's season. The Panthers went on to win six of their next seven games. With a 7–8 record heading into the final week of the season, a win against the New Orleans Saints would give the injury-ridden Panthers a chance to make the playoffs.

Twice New Orleans took an 11-point lead. Each time, Delhomme threw a touchdown pass to Muhammad and brought the Panthers back in the game. Then with 50 seconds remaining and trailing

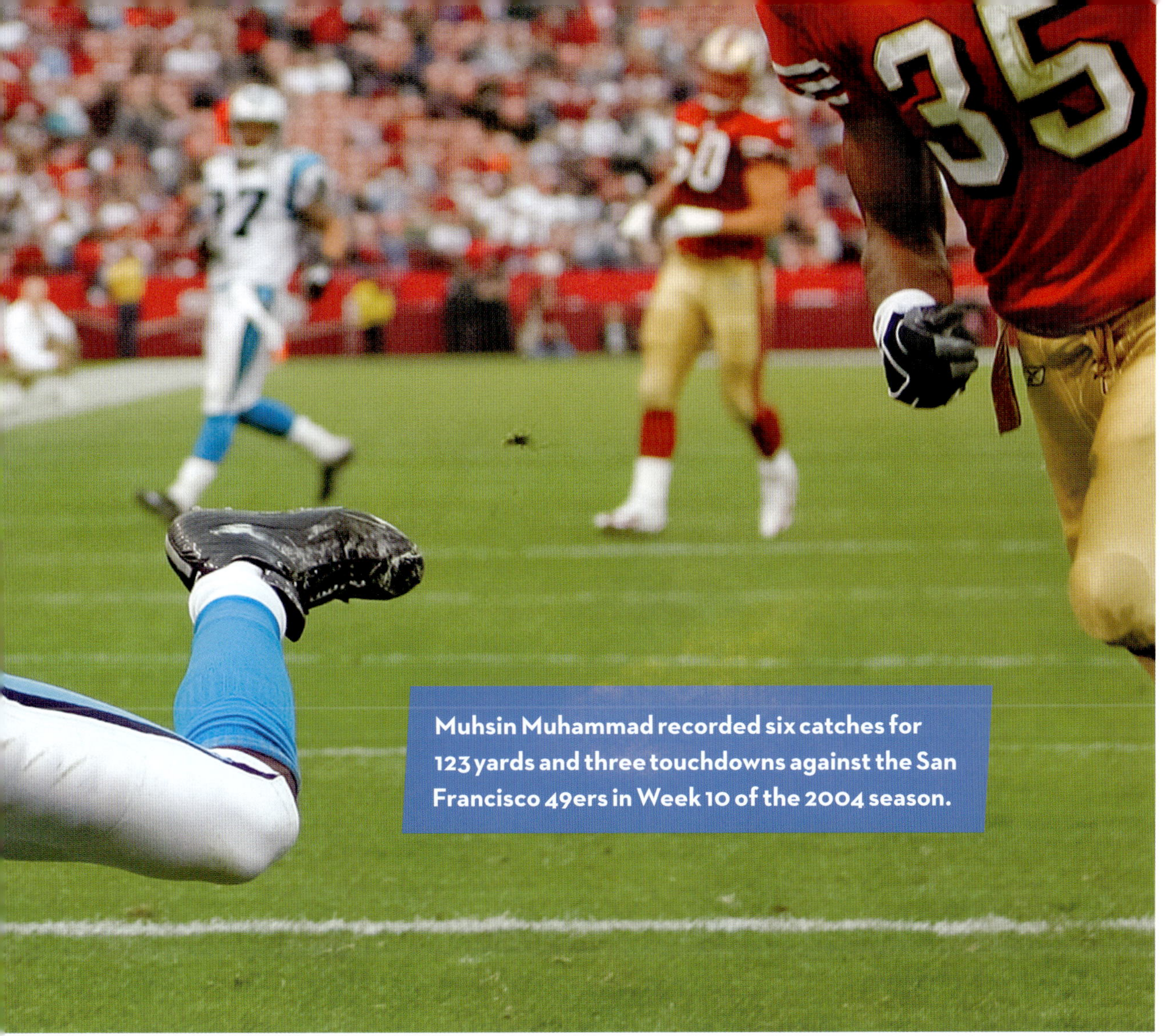

Muhsin Muhammad recorded six catches for 123 yards and three touchdowns against the San Francisco 49ers in Week 10 of the 2004 season.

21–18, the Panthers started a drive on their own 2-yard line. Carolina's season was on the line. Just as he had done all season, Delhomme looked to Muhammad. The receiver caught back-to-back passes to bring the Panthers past midfield. With time running out, the Panthers lined up for a field goal. However, the Saints blocked it to end their season.

A STAR RETURNS

Muhammad led the NFL with 1,405 receiving yards and 16 receiving touchdowns in 2004. But the following year, the Panthers didn't want to pay Muhammad his bonus. So the team cut him and he signed with the Chicago Bears.

Without Muhammad, the Panthers looked to the now-healthy Smith to reassert himself as the team's star receiver. He did that and then some, leading the NFL with 103 receptions, 1,563 receiving yards, and 12 receiving touchdowns.

With an 11–5 record, the Panthers returned to the playoffs. Smith's stellar play carried into the postseason. In the wild-card round, Smith scored two touchdowns and sealed a 23–0 victory over the New York Giants. The win set up a divisional round matchup in Chicago between the Panthers and their former star Muhammad.

The New Orleans Saints block John Kasay's late field-goal attempt during Week 17 of the 2004 season.

Chicago finished the season as the top team in its conference thanks to a suffocating defense. The Panthers and Bears had met in Week 11 of the regular season. Though Smith finished with 14 catches and 169 yards, the Bears picked off Delhomme twice and

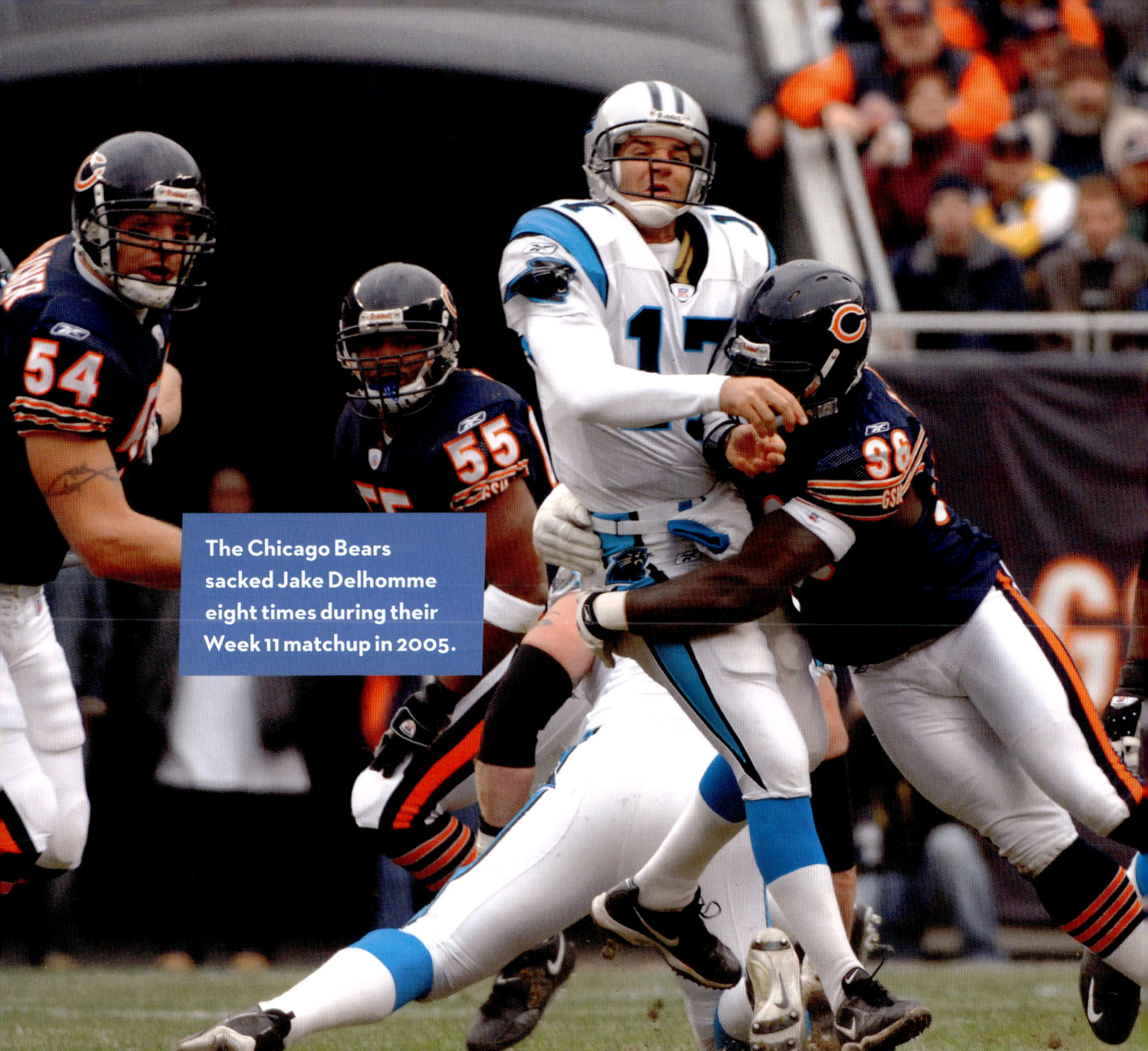
The Chicago Bears sacked Jake Delhomme eight times during their Week 11 matchup in 2005.

sacked him eight times in a 13–3 win. When the teams met again in the divisional round, Smith was determined to avenge the loss.

Less than a minute into the game, he ran past a Chicago defensive back to catch a pass 40 yards downfield. He then stopped on a dime to avoid another defender before strolling into the end zone. Later in the first quarter, Delhomme tossed another bomb to Smith deep downfield. With a defensive back draped over him,

Smith wrestled for the ball while falling down. He made the catch for a gain of 46 yards.

The Panthers jumped out to a 13–0 lead. But the Bears responded to make it a 16–14 game midway through the third quarter. That's when Smith struck again. On second-and-20, Smith streaked open down the field after a Bears defender fell down trying to cover him. A wide-open Smith easily scored a 39-yard touchdown to put the Panthers up by nine. Smith finished the 29–21 win with 218 receiving yards, a Carolina playoff record, to keep his dominant season going. In the next round, Smith and his team fell to the Seattle Seahawks.

Smith leaps to grab a pass over a defender. He is known for his incredible plays.

END OF AN ERA

The Panthers had struggled to find a consistent quarterback before Delhomme took over in 2003. Despite being signed as a backup,

Smith celebrates after scoring his second touchdown in a playoff game against the Bears after the 2005 season.

Delhomme brought stability to the position. After constantly feeding Smith during the 2005 season, Delhomme made his first Pro Bowl. However, he followed that up with a disappointing 2006 season in which he missed three games due to injuries. Then an elbow injury ended his 2007 season after three games. Carolina's consistent starter was starting to fade.

Delhomme rebounded in 2008. He helped the Panthers go a perfect 8–0 at home and win their division. The Panthers opened their playoff run with a home game against an Arizona Cardinals team that was in the playoffs for the first time in a decade. When Panthers running back Jonathan Stewart scored a little more than three minutes into the game, the rout seemed to be on.

A Cardinals defender leaps to bat down Delhomme's throw during a 2009 playoff game.

The inexperienced Cardinals didn't panic, though. After tying the game 7–7, they forced Delhomme to fumble at his own 13-yard line. On Carolina's next possession, Delhomme drove the offense down the field. Then he underthrew Smith for an easy Arizona interception. Later in the half, Delhomme threw into double coverage and turned the ball over once again. After a promising start, the Panthers headed into the locker room at halftime trailing 27–7.

Delhomme threw three more interceptions in the second half. No player had ever turned the ball over six times in a playoff game before. Following a 33–13 loss, Delhomme put the blame on himself, saying, "I didn't give us a chance tonight."

"I DIDN'T GIVE US A CHANCE TONIGHT."

—JAKE DELHOMME

Delhomme's terrible performance carried into the 2009 season. He turned the ball over five times in a Week 1 loss. Through 11 games, Delhomme threw eight touchdowns and 18 interceptions. A broken finger then ended Delhomme's year. After the season, the Panthers cut Delhomme. For the first time since 2003, Carolina was looking for a new starting quarterback.

A NEW HOPE

The Panthers selected quarterback Jimmy Clausen in the second round of the 2010 NFL Draft. In 10 starts that season, Clausen won only one game and threw seven interceptions. Securing only two wins all year, Carolina received the first pick in the 2011 draft. Teams usually don't draft quarterbacks with high picks in back-to-back years. But the Panthers couldn't pass up the chance to take Cam Newton.

Coming into the 2010 college

EMOTIONAL GOODBYE

After the Panthers cut Jake Delhomme in 2010, the team held a press conference to give him a chance to say goodbye to fans. Delhomme didn't hold back his emotions while talking to the media. He paused multiple times to wipe tears off his face. Delhomme wasn't sad though. He told the media those were tears of joy. He said he was thankful to the team for taking a chance on a "nobody" and letting him play quarterback in the NFL.

Delhomme wipes away tears during his final press conference with the Panthers.

football season, no one expected Newton to be a high draft pick. But in his only season at Auburn, he led the team to a perfect 14–0 record and a national championship. He also won the Heisman Trophy, which goes to the best player in college football. After Newton's dominant season, the Panthers nabbed him to be their new franchise quarterback. Newton had a rare combination of arm strength, size, and athleticism. With a 6-foot-5, 245-pound frame, he could run over small defenders. And he had the speed to easily pass bigger ones.

Cam Newton ran for 1,473 yards during his one season at Auburn.

Newton didn't disappoint in his NFL debut. On the third pass attempt of his pro career, Newton launched a deep pass to Smith for a 77-yard touchdown. Just before halftime, Newton lobbed a perfectly placed pass to Smith in the back of the end zone for a touchdown. In the second half, Newton dived from the 3-yard line

Newton dives into the end zone for the first rushing touchdown of his career.

to score another touchdown. On top of Newton's three touchdowns, he finished the game with 422 passing yards. That set a record for most passing yards in a player's first NFL game. While the Panthers ended up losing 28–21, it was clear that they had a star in the making.

Cam Newton threw for a career-high 4,051 yards during the 2011 season.

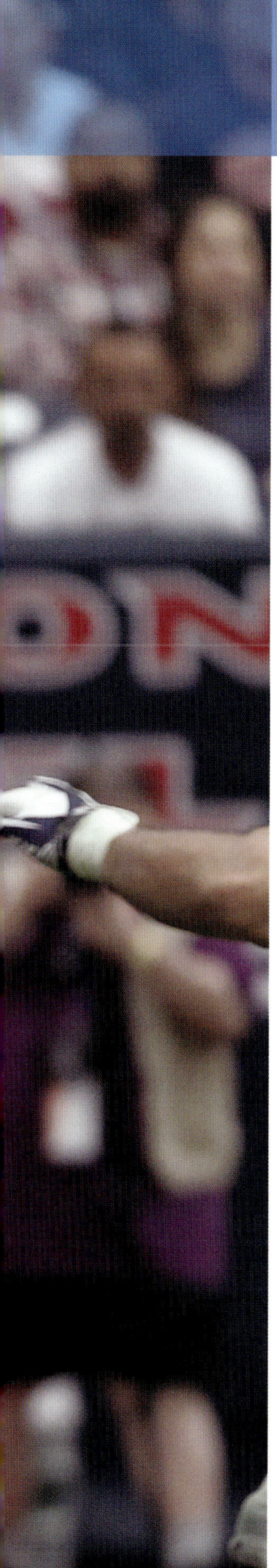

CHAPTER 5

ELITE TALENT

The Panthers immediately started building a strong team around Cam Newton. After drafting him, Carolina traded for Chicago Bears tight end Greg Olsen. The Panthers also hired Ron Rivera as their new head coach. He became known for his tendency to take chances on fourth down.

Newton continued his stellar play throughout the 2011 season. He threw for more than 4,000 yards. Newton also threw 21 touchdowns. The media voted him the NFL Offensive Rookie of the Year by a landslide.

Then in the 2012 draft, the Panthers selected linebacker Luke Kuechly in the first round. Kuechly racked up tackles by quickly shutting down running lanes. And he was equally skilled at reading a quarterback's eyes to pick off passes. Leading the league in tackles, Kuechly claimed the NFL Defensive Rookie of the Year Award. In his second year, he won the NFL Defensive Player of the Year Award.

NEARLY PERFECT

With their two young stars leading the way, the Panthers won their division in 2013 and 2014. Then everything came together in 2015. By his fifth NFL season, Newton had developed into the most dangerous offensive player in the league. Defenses always had to worry about his running ability, which left open space for his receivers. And when the Panthers got near the goal line, stopping Newton from jumping into the end zone seemed impossible.

The Panthers started the 2015 season 13–0. Another win looked certain when Newton threw five touchdowns to give the Panthers a 35–7 lead over the New York Giants. But the Giants stormed back. New York wide receiver Odell Beckham Jr. caught a touchdown to tie the game with 1:46 left. After Beckham Jr.'s touchdown, a camera caught Newton calmly nodding his head before going to grab his helmet. He knew there was plenty of time for him to win the game. Newton then led the Panthers down the field to set up a 43-yard field-goal attempt. Carolina's Graham Gano

Luke Kuechly recorded 1,092 tackles during his eight seasons with Carolina.

Greg Olsen reaches to catch a touchdown against the Seahawks in a playoff game after the 2015 season.

made the kick and kept the Panthers undefeated at 14–0.

The Panthers finished the season 15–1. Newton led the highest-scoring offense in the league. He easily won the NFL Most Valuable Player (MVP) Award.

In their playoff opener, the Panthers jumped out to a 31–0 lead before beating the Seattle Seahawks 31–24. Carolina put on a dominant display in the conference championship game against the Arizona Cardinals. Newton passed for more than 300 yards while throwing for two touchdowns and running for two more. Meanwhile, the Panthers' defense created seven turnovers. Kuechly sealed the 49–15 win with a pick six, sending Carolina to the Super Bowl.

The Panthers faced the Denver Broncos in Super

SUPER CAM

Cam Newton has been called "Superman" for as long as he can remember. That nickname inspired his go-to touchdown celebration. After scoring a rushing touchdown, Newton would put two fists together on his chest and then spread them apart. This replicated what Clark Kent, Superman's secret identity, would do to take on the role of Superman. Kent would rip off his shirt to reveal the Superman costume underneath his clothes.

The Denver Broncos' Von Miller, *right*, knocks the ball out of Newton's hand during Super Bowl 50.

Bowl 50. While Carolina had the league's highest-scoring offense, the Broncos possessed the league's best defense. Denver's crushing defense was led by star outside linebacker Von Miller. The Broncos had selected Miller one pick after the Panthers took Newton in 2011.

Early in the Super Bowl, Miller sprinted past a helpless offensive lineman to sack Newton and force the ball out of his hands. The Broncos fell on the fumble in the end zone to take a 10–0 lead. Miller and the Denver defense continued to give Newton trouble all game. The Broncos won 24–10, ending Carolina's commanding run.

OFFENSIVE WEAPON

The Panthers struggled to find success in 2016 and missed the playoffs. With the eighth pick in the next year's draft, the Panthers selected Christian McCaffrey. The running back was coming off two stellar seasons at Stanford. His combination of speed and agility made him tough to bring down in the open field. And McCaffrey also possessed great route-running skills out of the backfield. However, his 5-foot-11, 210-pound frame had some fans worried he wasn't big enough to handle the physicality of the NFL.

The Panthers eased McCaffrey into the league as a runner. But they used him heavily in the passing game right away, and he quickly became one of Newton's favorite targets. In his rookie year, McCaffrey caught 80 passes for 651 yards. Adding the all-around weapon helped the Panthers return to the playoffs. However, they lost to the New Orleans Saints in the wild-card round.

McCaffrey quickly developed into one of the league's most explosive players. In 2019, he led the NFL in yards from scrimmage and total touchdowns. But as McCaffrey was ascending, the Panthers began to fall apart.

Christian McCaffrey had a knack for escaping defenders' attacks.

A NEW ERA

The Panthers were nearing the end of a successful season on the field in 2017.

But many issues were taking place off the field. In December 2017, *Sports Illustrated* magazine published a story with details about how Panthers owner Jerry Richardson had acted inappropriately while running the team. It specifically accused Richardson of harassing multiple women coworkers and using a racial slur toward a team scout. The day the story came out, Richardson announced that he would be selling the team.

McCaffrey recorded 2,392 yards from scrimmage and 19 touchdowns in 2019.

In July 2018, businessman David Tepper bought the Panthers for $2.2 billion. Shortly after buying the team, he announced his plans to build a new practice facility. It seemed as if the Panthers were headed back in the right direction.

But they struggled on the field. The usually durable Olsen started to suffer frequent injuries. Then in 2019, Newton suffered a season-ending foot injury two weeks into the season. Rivera kept the team competitive, and the Panthers won five of their next six games without Newton. However, the Panthers lost four games in a row after that. Tepper fired Rivera before the end of the season.

Tepper knew it would take some time to turn his team back into a contender. He gave head coach Matt Rhule a seven-year contract to do it. It was an unconventional choice. Though Rhule had enjoyed success at Baylor University, he had never led an NFL team. Tepper expressed confidence in his new coach. However, the Panthers struggled to just five wins in 2020 and 2021 as McCaffrey battled injuries both seasons. After a 1–4 start in 2022, Tepper fired Rhule.

A little more than a week later, the Panthers traded McCaffrey to the San Francisco 49ers in exchange for four future draft picks. The team became committed to fully rebuilding its roster.

Newton left Carolina after the 2019 season. Though he came back in 2021, he played in only eight games before the team moved on again. The Panthers struggled to find

Ron Rivera had a record of 76-63-1 in nine seasons with the Panthers.

PANTHERS TROPHY CASE

SUPER BOWL CHAMPIONSHIPS: 0

CONFERENCE CHAMPIONSHIPS: 2

2003, 2015

DIVISION TITLES: 6

NFC West: 1996
NFC South: 2003, 2008, 2013, 2014, 2015

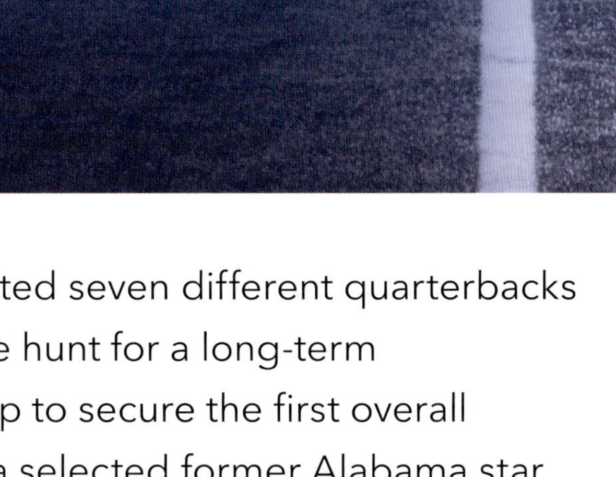

All stats are through the 2024 season.

a consistent quarterback. They started seven different quarterbacks from 2019 through 2022. Still on the hunt for a long-term quarterback, the Panthers traded up to secure the first overall pick in the 2023 NFL Draft. Carolina selected former Alabama star Bryce Young.

Young's rookie season did not go as planned. Because the team traded away top receiver D. J. Moore to get Young, the quarterback had few reliable targets to throw to. The Panthers' offensive line struggled to block for Young or any of the team's running backs. And Young's lack of size seemed to be an issue in the NFL. The low point of the season came in Week 17. With the Panthers down 26–0 against the Jacksonville Jaguars, Young threw an interception to seal the loss. Tepper attended the game and became so angry that he threw a drink at a Jaguars fan. The NFL fined Tepper $300,000 for his actions.

Heading into the 2024 season, the Panthers had hope that Young could overcome his disappointing rookie season. However, following the quarterback's struggles in two blowout losses, new head coach Dave Canales benched him. The time off helped Young. He started Carolina's final 10 games of 2024 and led the team to a 4–6 record while scoring 20 total touchdowns in that span. Despite the rough start to his career, Young looked like a quarterback the Panthers could build their team around.

Bryce Young threw for 2,877 yards and 11 touchdowns in 2023.

TIMELINE

1995
The Panthers play their first NFL season.

1996
Carolina wins its division and its first playoff game, defeating the Dallas Cowboys 26–17.

2002
After finishing with a 1–15 record, the Panthers hire John Fox as their new head coach and draft Julius Peppers with the second overall pick.

2003
Carolina signs Jake Delhomme prior to the season, and he leads the team on a run to Super Bowl XXXVIII.

2005
A year after breaking his leg, Steve Smith leads the NFL in receptions, receiving yards, and receiving touchdowns.

2008
Despite going undefeated at home in the regular season, the Panthers lose 33–13 to the Arizona Cardinals in a home playoff game.

The Panthers select Cam Newton with the top pick in the draft.

2011

2013

Luke Kuechly wins the Defensive Player of the Year Award and helps the Panthers win their division for the first time in five years.

Newton wins the MVP Award and leads the Panthers to Super Bowl 50.

2015

2018

David Tepper buys the Panthers.

Christian McCaffrey records 2,392 yards from scrimmage and 23 total touchdowns, leading the NFL in both categories.

2019

2020

Kuechly retires from the NFL with 1,092 career tackles.

GLOSSARY

clinch–when a team secures something, such as a win or a playoff berth.

contract–an agreement to play for a certain team.

debut–first appearance.

double coverage–when two defenders cover the same receiver.

draft–a system that allows teams to acquire new players coming into the league.

expansion team–a new team that is added to an existing league.

fine–when someone pays an amount of money as a punishment.

franchise quarterback–a quarterback capable of leading a team for a number of years.

free agent–a player who is not signed to a team.

interception–a pass that is caught by a defensive player.

pick six–an interception returned for a touchdown.

play-action–a play in which the quarterback fakes a handoff before dropping back to pass.

pocket–the area behind the line of scrimmage where the quarterback stands after dropping back to pass.

retire–to end one's career.

rookie–a professional athlete in his or her first year of competition.

roster–a list of players who make up a team.

route–a set path a receiver runs during a play to get open.

sack—a tackle of the quarterback behind the line of scrimmage before he can pass the ball.

safety—a score of two points for a team when its opponent is unable to advance the ball out of its own end zone.

turnover—loss of the ball to the other team through an interception or fumble.

veteran—someone who has played for many years.

ONLINE RESOURCES

Booklinks
NONFICTION NETWORK
FREE! ONLINE NONFICTION RESOURCES

To learn more about the Carolina Panthers, please visit **abdobooklinks.com** or scan this QR code. These links are routinely monitored and updated to provide the most current information available.

INDEX